D1101490

VII:
DAVID
BECKHAM

EVESHAM COLLEGE
796.334
LIBRARY
31036

WITHDRAWN

Evesham & Malvern Hills College
Library
31036

VII: DAVID BECKHAM

PHOTOGRAPHY BY DEAN FREEMAN + WORDS BY AMY LAWRENCE

WEIDENFELD & NICOLSON

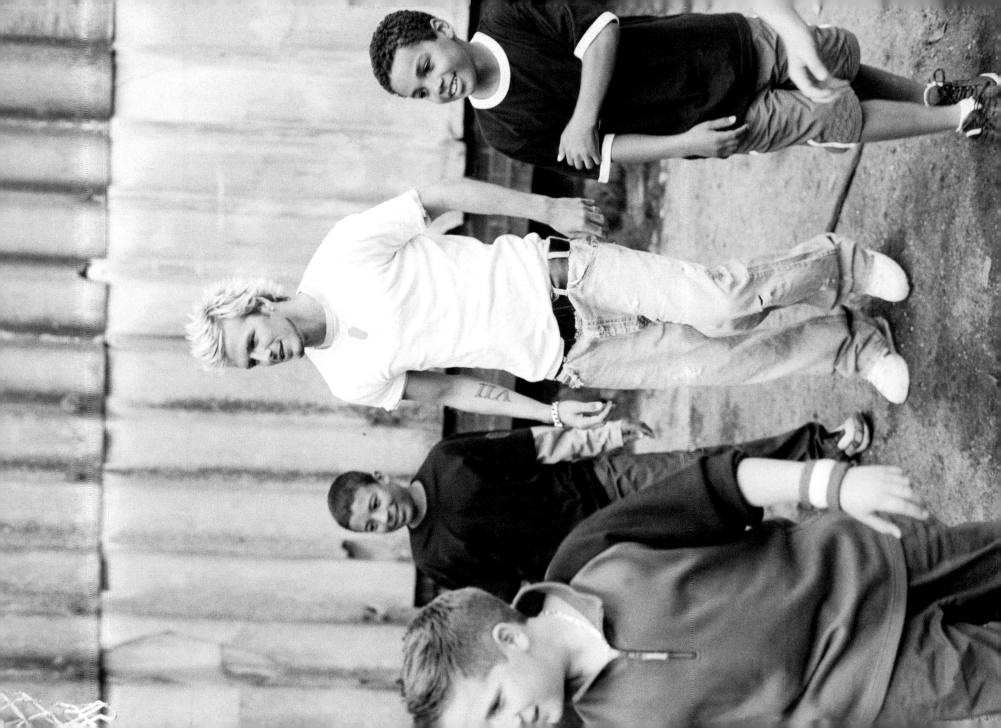

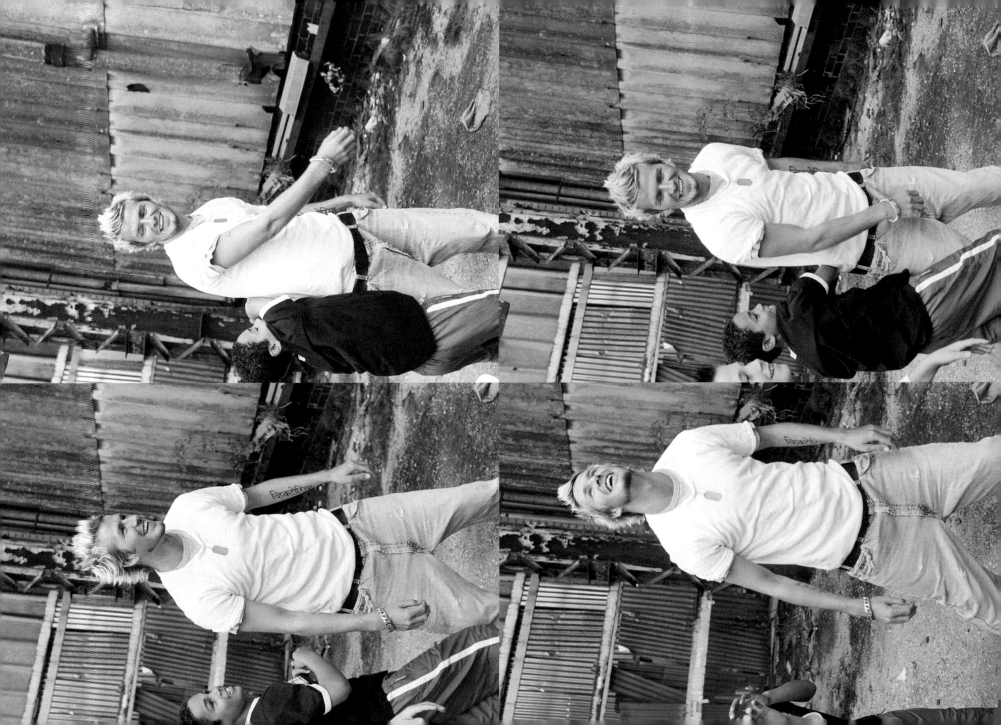

JOHN, AGED 13, LONDON. Wants to be Beckham. Wants the life. Wants the cash, the cars, the cool, the clothes. Oh, and to be a footballer. What a cushy life.

MARIA, AGED 49, MADRID. Wants to mother Beckham. What a sweet, handsome boy, and such a determined player.

ALFIE, AGED 27, LAGOS. Wants to talk about Beckham. At length, and with remarkable fervour and knowledge. The big question he wants answering is, should England play him on the right or in the centre? What were they thinking with this libero role?

ALEX, AGED 64, MANCHESTER. Wants to avoid talking about Beckham. At all costs. Shut it. The subject is taboo considering the fact is United, the boy's former club, evidently miss him more than he would ever contemplate admitting.

NAOKO, AGED 11, OSAKA. Wants to love Beckham. Posters adorn the walls, and the face fuels the romantic fantasies. A dreamboat.

GEORGIE, AGED 22, NEW YORK. Wants to get that body on the cover of his futuristic fashionista magazine. Beckham is happy to be a gay icon don't you know. And he will make the boys drool, darling.

JACK, AGED 58, STADIUM PRESS BOX ANYWHERE IN THE WORLD. Wants to see Beckham fall, fail, flounder. The bile is constantly flowing. All that extra-curricular activity is a stain on the Corinthian ideals of sport, just who the devil do he and his dreadful entourage think they are?

ROMEO, AGED 3, PLAYING IN THE GARDEN. Wants to sprint over to daddy as fast as his little legs will carry him.

EXCLUDING HERMITS AND THE PLANET'S MOST ISOLATED TRIBES, the words 'David Beckham' always provoke reaction. Regardless of gender, age, creed, religion, nationality or sexual preference, nobody ever says: 'Who?'

At the epicentre of his own global phenomenon, there's no question it must be weird to the point of absurd being Beckham. Imagine, outside of the confines of your own home, everybody stares. Everybody points. Everybody talks. Everybody wants. In the radar of footballers who are far less famous than Beckham, it's not unusual to see fans follow their heroes into a restaurant's toilets to bang on the door and shriek their name, or newspapers sling enough mud to leave someone in it up to the neck. Chasing, ranting, stalking, come with the territory. And in Beckham's world, it's multiplied to the maximum.

As his critics note (often and loudly) he is well rewarded for the inconvenience, and the perks of the job – such as being the world's richest footballer – cannot be too onerous a burden to bear.

But there is another price Beckham pays for his celebrity, one which arguably frustrates him more than the incessant demands of the public: beneath the thick veneer of his carefully manicured image lies what appears to be a fairly simple boy from Leytonstone who is in love with football and is committed to doing his best. Yet he is judged on different criteria to just about any of his contemporaries. A bad performance, a red card, a missed penalty, require national debate, hysterical polemics and, occasionally, a full-blown character assassination.

Beckham the footballer exists in the context of Beckham the brand. How many shirts he sells has become as crucial a statistic as how many crosses find a team-mate. As Pele once remarked, 'He is more of a pop star than a player these days.' And that's precisely why the world is fascinated with him to a degree so utterly disproportionate to his day job. Sometimes it must make him want to tear that exquisitely styled hair out.

He broke the mould. He was the right face at the right time to symbolize the moment the football landscape was transformed at the turn of the last century. At first we sniggered when Ruud Gullit coined the phrase 'sexy football'. But truth be told, these days the game doesn't seem to mind metaphorically showing a bit of cleavage if there is hard cash to be made. Clubs, players, matches, merchandising, and even loyalty – everything's for sale to the highest bidder.

While old-fashioned sporting values and working-class roots have been withering, dying out, new commercial empires have sprouted up all over the place. As one Premiership footballer exclaimed of Old Trafford once the stadium grew, the car parks mushroomed, the megastores opened their doors to the masses, 'It's not a football ground these days, it's a city.'

Had Beckham been born even ten years earlier, before football's big boom, his status would not have spread too far outside the confines of the back pages of newspapers in England. In 1999 Becks was part of Manchester United's Treble-winning team and already a multi-millionaire. It was the stuff of legend, and the players were priceless. Rewind a decade and in 1989 British clubs were banned from Europe as a consequence of hooliganism culminating in the death of 39 fans at the Heysel disaster. Arsenal, who won the Championship that season, paid some of their players £200 per week.

In 2003, Beckham's £20 million transfer from Manchester United to Real Madrid was the hottest story of the summer. His medical was televised live, and reportedly generated the second biggest TV audience after Diana's funeral. His unveiling press conference was a major event for the international press. In 1993, United's most lucrative sale was Danny Wallace to Birmingham for £250,000.

In 2004, Rebecca Loos earned herself a fortune and fame by association when her story of liaisons with Beckham seized the headlines for weeks on end. In 1994, your average football scandal involved brown envelopes, and dodgy meetings at motorway service stations to discuss transfer fees. Footballers' wives, or girlfriends, seldom even stirred local interest. Loos, lest we forget, earned £1 million for a one-hour kiss and tell television interview on Sky News. Even Becks does well to take that sort of money home for an hour's work.

This is football in the early twenty-first century. Old school versus new cool. It all came to a head – Beckham's head to be precise – on 15 February 2003. After an unpalatable defeat in the FA Cup against Arsenal, the scapegoat chosen to bear the brunt of manager Sir Alex Ferguson's rage was Manchester United's most glamorous player. The Scot is a charismatic overlord famed for ruling his club with an iron will few dare to question. But something inside Beckham snapped, and David dared to go for Goliath. In a flash of spectacular pique, Ferguson lashed out at a boot lying on the floor of the dressing room deep in the bowels of Old Trafford. The boot hurtled through the air and thwacked Beckham just above the eye. Fury, blood, stitches, and an obviously welcome opportunity for the paparazzi to record the occasion made for an extravagant scandal.

It was also a defining moment in modern football. In the red-faced corner, Sir Alex Ferguson represented the traditional values of the people's game, where respect and discipline underpin the running of the club, and where there is no 'I' in team. In the red-eyed corner, David Beckham, with his celebrity wife, advertising contracts, fashion-conscious dedication to haircuts, and a personal fortune to far outstrip the man paid to give him instructions, represented player power. It is an unwritten law in football that no player is bigger than any club. No player is bigger than any manager. Beckham's status challenged that fundamental truth. The flying boot was about far, far more than bowing out of the FA Cup.

It turned out to be a Zeitgeist moment in the evolution of football from working-class sport to the millionaire's playground. That Beckham was the catalyst was entirely appropriate.

The photograph splashed over the front pages of the newspapers was dynamite. The most famous face of his generation scarred. And his reaction to the scandal? Classic Beckham. There was a hint of the stubborn rebel – he chose to expose his stitches to the world, discarding what had become a trademark big hat pulled down over his head to ensure the stitches were unmissable to even a long lens. But he wasn't rebel enough to embark upon a public slanging match with his famously ruthless manager. Despite the elocution lessons and intensive PR training which have helped him to converse with more confidence, even he's not that stupid.

While the battle rumbled on for a while, Beckham eventually won the war when he was sold. Of the three parties involved in the deal – United, Real Madrid, and the player himself – there is not much doubt about who came off worst. While none of them is quite the force they once were, only one of them is hampered by £300 million-worth of debt.

Manchester United have had all sorts of issues to deal with since a critical phone call in the summer of 2003 between then Chief Executive Peter Kenyon and the club's star attraction made it pretty clear that United were eager to get on with life after Beckham. For the man himself, who had been fanatical about the club for as long as he could remember, that was like being served with divorce papers he never expected. A slap in the face? Maybe. But the evidence suggests United still feel the sting in their fingers all these years later.

Since Beckham's departure the trophy cabinet at Old Trafford has been relatively barren, the company has been sold to American investors who are using its income to service huge debts, and they have had to accept being elbowed off the top table both at home and on the Continent. When the going has got tough, it's easy to wonder whether Beckham's stream of crosses for Ruud van Nistelrooy, his sweetly struck corners and free kicks, and his remorseless determination might – just might – have got them going occasionally.

With Beckham it has always been easy to underestimate the footballer because of the face. Perhaps that explains why proving people wrong is one of the impulses which pumps blood fastest through his veins.

It must confuse him sometimes when he is condemned for using football to fuel his celebrity. Or condemned for using celebrity to fuel his football. He was just a handsome lad with talent in his feet, and if companies wanted to pay him more pounds than he could even add up with a calculator to advertise their products – which enabled him to enjoy the luxuries of life – well, who wouldn't?

It's worth pausing for a moment to emphasize how all this could only have happened to David Robert Joseph Beckham. Just as football took those all important steps out of its traditional heartlands and stormed into the realms of business, marketing, showbiz, he was the obvious choice to be cast as the male lead. Who else had catwalk looks, a pop star on his arm, a taste for glam, and he could play a bit, too? Who cares if he wasn't exactly a contender for University Challenge?

INTERVIEWER: *'Are you a volatile player?'*
BECKHAM: *'Well, I can play in the centre, on the right and occasionally on the left side.'*

DO WE EXPECT TOO MUCH OF OUR FOOTBALLERS? The columnist Julie Burchill struck a moot point when she observed, 'Much has been made of David Beckham's alleged dimness over the years – we don't expect our intellectuals to be great footballers, but for some reason we expect our great footballers to be intellectuals.'

Today a relatively comfortable (if steadfastly diplomatic) talker in his role as England captain, in his formative years Beckham was not known for his dazzling repartee.

The self-conscious young man thrust into the limelight sounded like he had his brains in his boots. At first this wasn't a major problem, but it started to become an issue the moment he became a household name. The halting, squeaky voice, and bouts of foot-in-mouth disease were at odds with the burgeoning Beckham image. Not very cool.

All of a sudden, after a summer break he returned to the scene with more confidence – not to mention more bass notes – in his delivery. Elocution lessons signalled how serious he was about presenting himself in as polished a manner as possible. Coincidence?

The Beckham phenomenon evolved because his rising star collided with the cosmos inhabited by Victoria Adams, better known as Posh Spice. Her influence on the rebranding of this handsome young footballer – and on the fact he wanted to dive headlong into the starry world she inhabited – was critical. Sweetly, Beckham once said that he would love his wife just as much if she worked in Tesco. But he was initially attracted to her precisely because she's a Harrods' girl.

What perfect media fodder: the relationship between the dumb blond footballer and the pouting pop singer whose group relished their role in taking a sledgehammer to gender barriers.

Before long the remodelled Beckham challenged the conventional footballer's image to the core. His chosen sport being a notoriously testosterone fuelled environment, photographs of him in a sarong, or wearing nail varnish, or with the arcs of his eyebrows delicately plucked, caused minor tremors around Fleet Street and beyond. He was evidently in touch with his feminine side – and Victoria stretched the point by joking in an interview that David wore her underwear.

On mainstream television, a popular parody of Posh and Becks became the highlight of a comedy show where impersonators created the impression that it wasn't necessarily the wonderboy who wore the trousers in the Beckham household.

Back at the training ground, Sir Alex Ferguson winced. Quite apart from how it looked, as far as he was concerned it represented a shift of concentration away from the parameters of the football pitch. The seeds of discontent in a relationship Beckham valued as a 'driving force' of his career were sown.

There are two words, not mentioned to him very often and only effective if spoken by those who know him well, which have the capacity to cut him right to the bone: 'You've changed.' He accepts his life has changed – access to whatever fashion whims his heart desires, a fleet of cars, luxury houses, a network of high security – but personality-wise?

In his autobiography *My Side*, when he tells of the courtship of his wife, Victoria, he confesses to being sentimental, old-fashioned, tongue-tied, nervous as hell, a bit clumsy. He doesn't mind mocking himself by admitting he wrote her phone number down numerous times on different pieces of paper just in case he should lose it. He sent her a red rose every day. It's hardly the illusion of the macho hunk which would later become so iconic. 'David changes nappies and he is very handy with the vacuum cleaner,' Victoria mischievously revealed later.

As it happens, his down to earth quality does nothing to undermine his image. It humanizes him. On the one hand we have the modern-day England captain who smoulders and postures to sell shirts, razors, sunglasses, mobile phones... On the other is the young man sitting at home on his mum's sofa flicking through the teletext to find he'd been picked to represent his country for the very first time. Somehow – and against all odds – he has retained an element of the run of the mill lad he was before global hysteria kicked in.

No amount of razzmatazz manages to completely conceal the sense of a nice, well brought up, ordinary sort. He has a natural warmth, he makes people who are expecting to be overwhelmed or unimpressed feel at ease, disarmed even. There is something Diana-esque about the way he tries to spread a little happiness when he meets the general public. The knockout smile, an arm around the shoulder, the common touch, is invariably a winner.

One of the most striking examples of this took place in the Estadio Bernebeu, on the day he was officially unveiled as Real Madrid's newest *galáctico*. A stage-managed debut public appearance was underway, with Beckham juggling the ball in front of his new fans, when a young boy dashed out of the seats and sped across the turf towards him. Club officials and security heavies tensed, only for Beckham to whisk the boy into his arms for a cuddle, and call for a Real Madrid shirt to pop over his little head.

For Real's head honchos watching this little interlude from the sidelines, it was PR heaven. Welcome to planet Beckham. This is a place where things happen which are beyond belief. Just a few months after he left for Madrid, a BBC poll found that 37 per cent of the British public believed David Beckham was more influential than God.

'Of all – hunger, misery, the incomprehension by the public – fame is by far the worst.'
— Pablo Picasso

IT WOULDN'T HAVE HAPPENED had he been born ten years earlier. It wouldn't have happened had he been ugly. It wouldn't have happened had he not married Posh Spice, one of the groundbreaking, newsmaking, girl-empowering group which briefly dominated popular culture and was the biggest selling act in the 1990s. There was something serendipitous happening, and from the moment everything came together the snowball rolled into overdrive.

Once Beckham entered the stratosphere of the super-famous, just about every area of his life was played out with the volume whacked up. Every event is taken to the extreme. Every disappointment becomes a crisis, every accomplishment a blazing triumph. Equilibrium doesn't figure.

Beckham's life fast turned into a modern-day morality play. Trace the key moments and it's easy to detect a definite pattern: from tribulation to redemption. There is something in his personality which almost invites ordeals, which duly set him up for moments of glorious salvation.

In the early days of his blossoming career, he seemed to have stumbled happily into the perfect life. Was he charmed? All he had ever wanted was to play football, his spiritual home was Old Trafford, and as a teenager he was recruited to learn his trade at the club he adored. He spent holidays training in Manchester, and once he reached 16 years of age, he was able to sign up as a trainee. Growing up, as a person and a player, with an elite group who turned out to be such an exceptional generation, Beckham and his friends collectively reached the pinnacle with their club, and played together for their country. For Fergie's fledglings, as they were known, life had a golden glow. The way that football has opened its boundaries and broadened its horizons since means that a bunch of close friends coming through at a major club together is unlikely to happen again. Beckham was lucky to be part of something so special.

His big break arrived with an audacious strike of his right foot in the dying minutes of United's first game of the 1996–97 season, at Wimbledon. He'd been around the first team for a year or so, but this moment one Saturday night catapulted him to the forefront of English football's imagination. Everybody interested in the game had been forewarned on the news. There was something sensational to watch on the television highlights. Something not to be missed. We all saw this blond boy inside his own half, when he looked up and sent the ball coasting halfway across the pitch, over the Wimbledon goalkeeper's head, and into the net. Beckham thrust out his arms in a celebration which would become familiar in the years to come. Later he would confess that, 'Hardly anything – for better, for worse – has been the same since.'

There was a lot of better before the first dose of worse kicked in. He met the woman he describes as the love of his life, became a regular with Manchester United and won trophies to boot, forced his way into the England team, and was picked to represent his country at the 1998 World Cup just after his twenty-third birthday. He had every excuse for thinking that this football lark was absolute paradise. It was a garden of Eden in which he was free to play to his heart's content.

The snake came suddenly. Brutally. England's World Cup journey reached its apex in a match so enthralling, at half time some onlookers were almost hysterical, pacing up and down the concourse inside the stadium, wittering like idiots. We knew we were witnessing a major event. The scene was set for the first major cataclysm in Beckham's career. England against Argentina is a contest with a peculiar temperature. It is one of the few international matches with the heat of a local derby, but without the geographical closeness to explain it. It is, by its specialist nature, as intense as it comes.

With the score locked at 2–2, the teams emerged for the second half with a classic there for the taking. Beckham's part in it ended abruptly when he reacted to some histrionics on the part of Diego Simeone by flicking a foot out at the Argentinian midfielder. The referee Kim Milton Nielsen brandished a red card and Beckham's role from thereon in was restricted to soul searching in the dressing room. England, with depleted numbers, eventually succumbed to Argentina in a penalty shoot out.

'Those 60 seconds will always be with me,' Beckham confessed, of the dramatic minute in which he tangled with Simeone, then referee Nielsen, and then his own tortured conscience.

The knock-on effect was, even by the standards of a media and public traditionally unforgiving of scapegoats, hardcore. 'Ten heroic lions, one stupid boy,' was a typical headline. Another daily newspaper printed his face on a dartboard. Elsewhere, on the streets, an effigy was hung from a lamp post, and there were death threats sent in the post. When football resumed its domestic routine after the summer's melodrama, all non-Manchester United football fans throughout Britain were apparently waiting for Beckham, and ready to vent their spleen.

He soon realized the worst part was feeling he brought suffering upon his family: 'My mum, dad, nan and granddad were reading and seeing things that upset them, and that was the most upsetting part for me,' he said. 'I was 23, and when people say the sort of things they were saying about me, you can either go home and cry, which I felt like doing because it was upsetting, or you come out fighting. Fortunately, I had people around me who made me come out and fight.'

Redemption would come in different stages. The first step was the welcoming, protective arm of his manager, Ferguson, and team-mates at Manchester United, which was echoed in the stands by supporters who saw it as a duty to defend their boy. Every time Beckham went to take a corner kick, United's fans would cheer him to the rafters. Beckham has never forgotten the relief applied so generously by the antidote to the hate brigade.

The next step came as United experienced a uniquely euphoric season. Hungrily hunting down silverware, their haul in 1999 of Premiership, FA Cup and Champions League marked an unprecedented success. The Treble culminated in a game which has become legend not for the verve with which United played (they were awful) but for their brilliant character. Losing 1–0 to Bayern Munich with the world watching and the clock almost up, they summoned a comeback, a never-say-die attitude, a refusal to be squashed, which beggared belief. Two quickfire goals turned football upside down. As somebody once said, last-minute goals are wonderful things. Especially when you don't deserve them.

For Beckham, less than 12 months after the Argentina debacle, the occasion marked a personal comeback too. What pleased him most was the way he turned things his own way through the sheer quality of his football. 'That has been the most rewarding thing for me. I could have done interview after interview, trying to explain myself, but instead I did it on the pitch, with the ball. I have worked hard to do it.'

Asked one day if he would do it all again differently, his reply is adamant. If you live with extremes, the troughs make the peaks even more resonant. The 1999 Treble would not have rocked him to the very core had he not withstood the hurricane of Argentina 1998.

'It is not a normal life for him.'
— Sven-Göran Eriksson, England manager

IN THE AFTERMATH OF THE ARGENTINA DISMISSAL, the atmosphere around his involvement with the national team tilted gradually from vindictive to lukewarm. By the time the next tournament came along, Euro 2000 in Holland and Belgium, Beckham was used to the stick he had to absorb. Much of it he put down to jealousy. Most of it was easily dismissed as irrelevant. He was not, however, easily able to ignore abuse aimed at his family. At the end of England's opening European Championship game in Holland, a 3–2 defeat to Portugal, Beckham heard some punters baiting him with nauseating comments about his wife and first son, Brooklyn. His retaliative gesture – middle finger raised in their direction – was caught on camera. Yet again, Beckham's temperament came under fierce scrutiny, although this time at least there was acknowledgement that some of his tormentors had overstepped the mark.

When he met up with England, tranquillity was hard to find. It is always a volatile environment, given that the level of pressure and expectation is heightened in a country which feels it has some sort of divine right to succeed because it is the birthplace of the sport. Beckham soon found himself even more involved. When Kevin Keegan quit as manager in the emotional maelstrom of the last match to take place beneath the twin towers of the ancestral home at Wembley, the atmosphere in the camp was particularly chaotic. What a moment for Beckham, of all people, to be made England captain.

He soon found a new ally in new coach Sven-Göran Eriksson. Both men who like the good things in life, who have made the most of their reputation, and who have had to endure heavy artillery from paper bullets, there is a kinship between them. Eriksson – like Beckham – may not have been everyone's leader of choice, but while England's World Cup qualification was on the line it made sense to give the new regime a chance to prove themselves. One scoreline in particular – Germany 1 England 5 – went a long way to achieving exactly that. Beckham's credibility as a captain soared after such a proud performance on the soil of old enemies.

But England's place at the 2002 World Cup remained in the balance until virtually the last kick of the qualification campaign. That kick fell to Beckham. It was a free kick – his speciality – against a Greek side already eliminated but enjoying the chance to plant a thorn in the bigshots' side. The game was at Old Trafford, his playground. A puff of the cheeks pumped him up for the kill, and he delivered.

Never was Beckham a more heroic figure.

In the calm after the storm, an hour or so after the game had finished and the crowds had jigged off to celebrate, Beckham walked through the still of the emptied out stadium. The handful of journalists left inside, some of whom had hounded him from time to time, stopped working to give him a standing ovation. Amazingly, that sight wasn't a hallucination.

His free kicks are refined enough to win admiration from the best of the best. Zico, a Brazilian maestro of dead ball arts, was impressed: 'His judgement of distance and power is amazing. Beckham is one of the best in the world at taking free kicks.'

And with that stunning strike against Greece, the 'stupid boy' who was lambasted for letting England down three years before became the man who transported them to the next World Cup.

If that free kick was another telling stride towards liberation from his Argentinian nemesis, the matter was dealt with once and for all a year later, at the finals, when the two old foes met for another passionate rendezvous. When England were awarded a penalty, Beckham momentarily felt his whole career had been building up to this seminal moment. He stood over the ball, and his old friend Diego Simeone stood in front of him. Fancy meeting again at a time like this.

Beckham struck the ball. Bingo. Finally, the chapter was closed.

'At last, there will be two good-looking players at the Bernebeu.'
— Roberto Carlos, Real Madrid and Brazil
    phenomenon of nature

ENGLISH FOOTBALLERS ARE NOT THE WORLD'S BEST TRAVELLERS. It is an anomaly, during an era when national and cultural barriers have fallen, and workers are freer than ever to ply their trade on foreign shores, that almost all the top English players remain at home. The Premiership hosts players from countless countries – they have come from Australia to Zimbabwe and anywhere in between – but exports are minimal.

Over the years, a select few British players have tried their luck abroad. Some fall into the Paul Gascoigne/Ian Rush category. In this case, the relationship between player and new country turns out to be one of mutual bafflement. Gascoigne's penchant for burping and farting was not a mode of communication widely used in Rome, while Rush famously described his spell in Turin as 'like living in a foreign country'.

Others, such as Gary Lineker and David Platt, prove that it is possible to quickly become fluent on and off the pitch. These players welcomed the opportunity to throw themselves into their new surroundings, and made positive impressions in Spain and Italy respectively.

Once it was announced Beckham was bound for Madrid his critics assumed he'd be more likely to fall into the Gascoigne/Rush trap than follow the Lineker/Platt example. He may be a trier but he is no linguist, and his lifestyle – not to mention his playing style – were hotly debated in both England and Spain before he had even kicked a ball in Real's colours.

In both countries, there were considerable misgivings. The writer John Carlin, in his book *White Angels*, observed how uninspired much of the Real fraternity was about

Beckham's impending arrival: 'The general view, and it extended to many fans, was that the Englishman was not a top-of-the-range Real Madrid player; that he had been bought to sell shirts and stick it up the old enemy, Barcelona. I know for a fact there were people high up the Real hierarchy who argued strongly against signing Beckham on precisely these grounds... And by the way, as men in bars were asking the length and breadth of Spain, wasn't he also a little bit of a *maricon* – a ponce? And what about this business, reported in the glossy magazine, of him wearing his wife's knickers? And those earrings, and the haircuts, and the Indonesian skirts...?'

Although the celebrity image which had become such anathema to Sir Alex Ferguson was actively embraced by the main man at Real, Florentino Perez, Beckham's feet evidently had to talk as impressively as the money he would make for his new club. On the pitch at the Bernebeu, Beckham had some serious convincing to do. Could he prove he was a footballer, not a clothes horse? Could he show he was a fighter, not a *maricon*?

In his debut at the Bernebeu, a Spanish Super Cup final against Real Mallorca, Beckham's personal scriptwriters intervened once again and provided a goal for him to savour and the sceptics to swallow.

It was typical Beckham. From doubt to deliverance in one dramatic swoop.

'Wretched the man whose fame makes his misfortunes famous.'
— Lucius Accius, poet born 170 BC

IN THE AREA OF EAST LONDON WHERE HE GREW UP, there is a 'Beckham trail', a walking route which takes in points of interest such as the house his grandparents lived in and the place he camped as a cub. Waltham Forest Council have helpfully included directions in Spanish and Japanese.

Britain's obsession with celebrity culture is a multi-million pound industry. In this era Beckham was the first to cross over from the sports pages. Up to a point, it must have made him feel invincible. Innovative, even.

The face of choice for every glossy magazine, Beckham was enthusiastic about the chance to blur the boundaries between football and fashion. It was often controversial. A homoerotic photo shoot and a narcissistic set of pictures styled on crucifix imagery took him into untouched territory for footballers. Then there was the lavish wedding – with *OK!* winning the bidding to publicize exclusive photographs with an eye-watering sum. The marriage took place in an Irish castle, with the bride and groom posing on matching purple thrones. Naturally, every detail of their romantic fantasy was analyzed and picked apart by the media.

On planet Beckham, the PR machine is at the ready 24/7. Whilst most footballers cherish the rare opportunity to put their feet up, let their hair down, and escape the spotlight, Becks spends summers on exhausting promotional tours to Asia and America with Posh.

He is such a marketable commodity, many of the brands he advertises don't need to present him as a footballer. When he models Police sunglasses, or shaves with a Gillette razor, what is important is the fact he is a handsome and recognizable face. An arresting sight. They don't need him to wear a kit or smash a football. Simon Fuller, the man who created the Spice Girls, believes the Beckhams can be more famous than the labels they are paid fortunes to promote. 'The combination of Victoria's glamour and David's sex appeal and sporting prowess could, over the long term, create a $1 billion brand,' he assessed. 'The Beckham brand is about aspiration and family values, the couple who came from nothing to achieve their dreams.'

As anybody who boards the celebrity rocket quickly discovers, there are no brakes on board. There is no emergency stop button. It is not possible to get off when the ride gets rocky. High fame in the twenty-first century is a Faustian pact. The price you pay for the riches and successes that come your way is this: in exchange you sell your freedom.

Much as they like to live in what they call 'bubble Beckham', the time they have in their sanctuary away from prying eyes, the family have left themselves vulnerable to extreme invasions of their privacy. The worst case involved plots to kidnap Beckham's wife and children. As a result, they now exist in a zone protected by top grade security at all times. The relationship between his football and his fame is never more painfully exposed than when his family is caught in the midst of a storm.

It has always been a double-edged sword. Dating to the early days of Beckham-mania, the influence Ferguson exerted on one part of his life, and Victoria exerted on the flipside, created a conflict. Controlling that struggle became a feature of his development as a person and a career man.

The morality-play image comes to mind again. Let's not dare to cast one as the good angel and the other as the bad, but the concept of Ferguson sitting on one shoulder and Victoria on the other, each tempting him with utterly opposing opinions, one pulling him towards football and the other towards fame, is not too far from the truth.

Evidently in awe of Ferguson throughout his junior years – he saw the Scot as a father figure and it was a standard dressing-room joke that Beckham was the manager's son – the relationship altered when David met Victoria. As Ferguson told *Sports Illustrated*: 'David was blessed with great stamina. The best of all the players I've had. After training, he'd always be practising, practising, practising. But his life changed when he met his wife. She's in pop and David got another image. He's developed this fashion thing. I saw his transition to a different person.'

Attempts to ruthlessly keep Beckham's starry lifestyle in check served only to rile the loved-up young footballer. When Beckham once missed a training session because his son was poorly, Ferguson's disapproval was caustic. 'You were babysitting while your wife was out gallivanting,' he quipped. Beckham was appalled. He didn't want to be torn between his wife and his manager, but caught between two such strong personalities, he somehow had to appease both.

Perhaps the traits he inherited from his parents, Ted and Sandra, held him in good stead. Beckham says he is 'as soft as mum and as stubborn as dad'. That balance wasn't enough, however, to keep the peace.

At Manchester United it became increasingly apparent that Ferguson was losing patience with the Beckham circus. A grinding friction led to another quake when the player was sensationally dropped from one of the most captivating matches on the calendar. In the Champions League, Real Madrid visited Old Trafford, and with whispers in football that Beckham might be a target for the Bernebeu club, it was an obvious blow below the belt to be named as a substitute. Not that it exactly kept him out of the limelight.

Soured relations between Ferguson and Beckham was the talk of football and the cameras were trained on both. But the PR had been taken care of – Victoria told David to wear a smile on the bench, to make sure he was not broadcast showing any negative emotions.

Obviously in turmoil inside, Beckham came off the bench in the second half to score with a trademark free kick and steal the headlines from a match which has become seminal in English football's modern history. It was the match which was glamorous and compelling enough to persuade a man called Roman Abramovich to invest some of his billions on this enthralling spectacle that so many people around the world love so much. That decision has taken football's relationship with money onto another level entirely. That Beckham provided the match's central storyline was somehow only natural.

The move to Madrid signalled a shift for bubble Beckham. Victoria's disinclination to live in Spain, as she preferred to stay at the Hertfordshire mansion affectionately known as Beckingham Palace, initially caused a strain. That turned into a scandal when Rebecca Loos, the PA hired to help him adjust to life in a new country, exposed his roving eye.

Having carved an identity as a devoted family man and proud England captain, Beckham's reputation unravelled. Loos's text sex sessions were followed by the story of Danielle Heath, who claimed to have provided 'full service' beauty treatments. It ensured the mass media devoured gossip about Beckham's marriage like ravenous vultures. There is precious little mystery about today's stars. Arguably, we know more intimate detail about Beckham than is strictly necessary.

Immediately after the revelations, his spin doctors were at work to redirect our attention to more palatable imagery: David and Victoria made themselves available for happy family photographs.

Going into his second season with Real, Beckham chose an interview on his club's in-house television station, Real Madrid TV, to publicly confirm his commitment to club and family. 'My wife, my family are happy. We're enjoying our lives here,' he said. 'We live here, this is where we want to bring our baby up and our two boys. My son Brooklyn is very happy at his school. He has a lot of friends there. He's coming home with something different every day, saying something different in Spanish and he seems very, very happy.'

Was his reputation damaged by extra-marital liaisons? Yes, but far from irretrievably. Although a series of well-orchestrated stunts were not enough to persuade the cynics that bubble Beckham was unbreakable, in time the mud washed off him. For whatever reason – because of his popularity? Because he's a football star? Because the ordinary Joe discussing it down the pub might have done the same given half a chance? Because he is charmed? – the mud just didn't stick. The flak bounced off him. His advertising contracts were not compromised. His adoring fans in Japan didn't forsake him. His family forgave him. 'Goldenballs' is an incredibly appropriate nickname.

'Beckham? His wife can't sing and his barber can't cut hair.'
— Brian Clough, self-styled footballing bighead

FRANKLY, ANYTHING LESS THAN A PITHY QUIP from the mouth of the incomparable Brian Clough would be a massive disappointment. But for most English people, a definition of David Beckham is a rather more complex issue.

If suddenly confronted with the question 'What do you think of Beckham?' it is not abnormal to be assailed with so many conflicting events, reactions, and themes, it's difficult to establish what to think. If you Google the words 'David Beckham' you get well over 4 million results. Think about Beckham we do, whether we like it or not. He is so ubiquitous in the social fabric it isn't that easy to get away from him.

An example. In the spring of 2002, Beckham broke a bone in his foot, which was the catalyst for a full-blown national crisis. The word metatarsal became a household expression the moment it was revealed that this was the bone in question, which had cracked after a heavy foul. Remember, metatarsal is a word seldom used outside podiatric specialists within the medical profession, but suddenly it was splashed all over the newspapers, was the talk of the television, expertly analyzed on the radio, and yakked about down the pub. The country was obsessed with metatarsals. What were they? How did they work? And most crucially of all, how long did they take to fix?!

An individual sportsman's individual injury can never have been so assiduously studied. In fairness that arguably says more about the British media, and the public, than Beckham. But inevitably, it didn't happen with anyone else (other players have been victim of the same affliction but prompted a mere fraction of the concern). It happened with him. And him alone.

In England, the build-up to the 2002 World Cup finals, a tournament which involves 736 players from around the globe, morphed into a countdown towards Beckham's full recuperation. If it wasn't so ludicrous it would be frightening.

The metatarsal obsession owed more to the fact he was an infamous player than an invaluable player. It also came with added spice because the villain who had inflicted the injury, Aldo Duscher, was Argentinian. It could only happen to Beckham.

'Beckham is unusual. He was desperate to be a footballer. His mind was made up when he was nine or ten. Many kids think that it's beyond them. But you can't succeed without practising at any sport.'
— Bobby Charlton, World Cup winner

THERE IS A MISCONCEPTION AMONGST YOUNG FOOTBALLERS who aspire to the Beckham lifestyle. The work ethic may not be number one on his fans' list of qualities, but it's a priority for the man himself. It was something instilled in him from his youth, when his father took him out and coached him as a toddler.

At his first club, Ridgeway Rovers, Beckham was smaller than many of the kids he played football with, and that only encouraged him to work harder still. The uncanny ability to strike a ball with wonderful pace and distance was always a hallmark – as a junior he was famed for manipulating the ball with remarkable consistency – but make no mistake he grafted at it. The fact that he enjoyed the graft, and still does, is an inbuilt part of Beckham's make-up. In fact, by the time he was settling in as a teenager with Manchester United, part of that graft was geared towards cutting out what the youth coach, Eric Harrison, referred to as 'Hollywood passes'. Beckham was a natural at them. He just had to learn when to use them and, just as crucially, when not to.

In this player power era, we are now in an age when a footballer showing off in a nightclub can burn £50 notes to prove how rich he is. Another who is demoted to the reserves because of indiscipline can taunt his manager by refusing to play, getting out his chequebook, and asking, 'How much is the fine?' Elsewhere a player whose head has been turned by the promise of greener grass can go on strike to manoeuvre a transfer. But one thing Beckham is not is unprofessional. In some ways he is a fan who never grew up, and his love for the game is undiminished by the years.

He always was an enthusiast, and never tired of practising. It is a trait he continues to this day, and it's the aspect of Beckham that has most surprised his employers and team-mates in Madrid. They thought they were buying a playboy, they couldn't believe they bought a workaholic.

In the physical tests that the club run to examine each player's individual performance, Beckham scores highly and is usually the player who has done the most running during 90 minutes. Whether that is sufficient to pass the *galáctico* test is an intriguing question.

Beckham's place in the *galáctico* culture is an interesting one. Florentino Perez, the Real Madrid President, strikes deals according to his vision that buying the most mythical players for the most fabled club would breed the most beautiful team imaginable. But was Beckham the obvious next stepping stone in an adventure that began with Luis Figo, moved on to Ronaldo, and then Zinedine Zidane? Figo, Ronaldo and Zidane had all been acclaimed as World Player of the year. They all arrived at Madrid as, arguably, the best of the best in the moment they were bought. Could the same be said of Beckham?

In terms of pure ability, God-given talent, the acquisition of Beckham was a deviation from the *galáctico* norm. His role as a team player was always more pronounced than the virtuoso soloists who Perez handpicked to precede him. They, more than he, could win games on their own. On the basis of pure talent, in the summer of 2003 Beckham was not the most attractive proposition at the sales. Not at a time when a certain Ronaldinho (who wraps up the World Player of the Year title almost unopposed these days) was up for grabs. That arch-rivals Barcelona have built a glorious team around the awe-inspiring Ronaldinho must, in private moments, make Perez think.

Beckham has other qualities, of course. Not least, a licence to print money that Ronaldinho (whose buck teeth and unruly hair prevent him from being an Adonis) cannot match. With a marketing boom in mind, the Beckham transfer was a major coup for Perez. It was estimated that the moment he joined, Manchester United lost almost a third of their 16 million Asian fans to Real Madrid in the time it takes to scribble a signature on a contract.

The figures were as startling as Perez hoped. Shirt sales of the famous white kit tripled once Beckham was modelling it. His number 23 shirt was the symbol of cool in the New York club scene that is as removed from the traditional football market-place as you can get. Television rights were sold more extensively, with Real's games being broadcast live to more countries than ever before. Perez defined Beckham as the final piece of the *galáctico* jigsaw, but the feeling persisted it was more of a commercial fit than a footballing one.

The acid question is this: would Real Madrid have bought a guy who played like Beckham but looked like Gary Neville? It was telling that during that momentous tie between the institutions of Manchester and Madrid, Beckham was the only United player on the pitch who was as famous as Real's *galácticos*.

The hard fact is that Beckham is the only trophy signing who didn't deliver the immediate return of silverware. Figo's first season was marked by Real reclaiming the La Liga title. Zidane arrived and won his new club the Champions League with a volley of stunning refinement in the final. Ronaldo came and helped Real to the title once again. Beckham marched into town... and the team ended the season with nothing.

Looking at the statistics, critics can choose to draw the conclusion that Beckham is the failing *galáctico*. But the statistics are misleading. Real's failure has been a collective one – bad management led to an unbalanced squad, bad coaching led to a rudderless team, bad performances led to too many squandered games.

Oddly, even though his period there has not yielded the number of trophies he, or the club, desire, Beckham has come out of it rather well. It is widely acknowledged that Real are enduring a difficult period because the legends they depend upon are showing signs of age, the decision to sack coaches at the average rate of two a season is not the wisest while there is instability in the team, and the policy of recruitment is off-kilter. The luxury players just keep on coming, while Claude Makelele, who was an indispensable anchor in midfield, has never been adqeuately replaced.

In the middle of this muddle, Beckham has won the admiration of Real's fans for his warrior spirit. They love his undimmable passion. They don't even curse him for the frequency with which he has been sent off, instead taking it as a sign of commitment.

Of his fellow *galácticos*, Figo was sold, Zidane has become increasingly peripheral, and Ronaldo has been jeered for showing more liking for a big dinner than the necessary fitness work required by a top athlete. Beckham has become a focal point of fans' adulation. They pin the blame for Real's struggles elsewhere. The coach. Perez. The other players. But Beckham is protected as if by the same magic forcefield which ensures he invariably comes out of any predicament smelling of roses – eventually.

Against their expectations, the Spanish have come to appreciate his footballing characteristics far more than they ever anticipated. And he appreciates the way he has had to improve his game to survive in La Liga. 'I've had to improve,' he said. 'It's a different league, a different type of football. In England it's more frantic, more intense. In Madrid you have a little more calm on the ball and your technique has to be perfect because all the way through La Liga the players are top quality.'

The newspaper *El Pais* had been among those who articulated general scepticism when he arrived in Spain: 'Beckham is a player for whom there is no need in this Real Madrid. Nothing that he does adds value to the team.' He might not be the *galáctico* of *galácticos*, but they were forced to eat their words all the same.

'He can't kick with his left foot, he can't head a ball, he can't tackle and he doesn't score many goals. Apart from that he's all right.'
— George Best, Manchester United's original glamour boy

BECKHAM WENT INTO 2006 looking forward to extending his commitment to Real Madrid and experiencing another World Cup adventure in Germany as captain of his country for the third successive tournament. He has clocked up over a half-century of armbands – a remarkable achievement. Only three Englishmen, Billy Wright, Sir Bobby Moore and Bryan Robson, have led the nation more often. Beckham often sprinkles the words 'honoured' and 'privileged' in his public speaking. On this occasion he is absolutely right.

He tries to emulate England's only World Cup-winning captain, saying once, 'I want to be liked like Bobby Moore. He was liked by all generations. There are players that have got that certain aura. Bobby Moore walked into a room and people stood up and clapped.'

Beckham is a controversial captain at times, and not everybody's cup of tea compared to the more orthodox leadership embodied in the likes of an uncompromising defender like John Terry. Beckham is more of a symbol than an organizer or a motivator.

He was able to challenge his own understanding of the role when a disagreement between the players and the Football Association threatened to turn into a serious diplomatic incident. When Rio Ferdinand, a team-mate of Beckham's at Manchester United, was dropped from international duty for a key England match in Turkey after failing to attend a drugs test, the squad threatened to boycott the match. Talk of mutiny rocked the camp as the players came out in sympathy with Ferdinand.

Beckham became a key link between the players and management, taking part in summit meetings and ensuring the game went ahead but the players' point was made. It was a role inconceivable around the time of the red card of Argentina 1998, and demonstrated how he had turned from hothead to pacifier.

On other occasions he has said or done the wrong thing. Admitting he took a strategic yellow card in an international match in order to serve a suspension at a convenient time was not the most brilliant of revelations. His record is further blemished by the red card he was shown during a World Cup qualifying match against Austria at Old Trafford in 2005. Dismissals for captains always lead to extra-loud questions about irresponsibility. And almost as damaging was the sight of the young tearaway Wayne Rooney swearing at his captain, and showing such obvious disrespect, during a dismal defeat in Northern Ireland.

Part of the media's hostility towards Beckham is rooted in his celebrity. But he remains rooted in the game. For that reason, his post-career thoughts are more about the soccer academies he has opened in Britain and the USA, than hanging up his boots to develop the empire that will doubtless continue to keep him in the manner to which he has become accustomed. Supporting the sport's grass roots is something which seems to genuinely enthuse him. He may enjoy being a model, but he is serious about his work as a role model.

Over the years he has been called many things. Goldenballs. The richest footballer in England. The most famous face in the world. Becks. Forrest Gump. Skipper. Bimbo. Wonderboy with the wondergoal. And to some, just plain David.

The Beckham phenomenon is a product of the times – and they are times he was the catalyst in bringing about.

Even George Best, even Eric Cantona, wouldn't have been idolized by a teenage girl in a provincial town in Japan.

There seem to be no limits to his fame. How many other icons would be featured in an art installation which presents a video of themselves sleeping? Exhibited by the National Portrait Gallery, Sam Taylor-Wood's uncut, one hour and seven minutes of film of Beckham in bed, alone, naked and fast asleep drew curious crowds from all over the world and a wide social spectrum. The artist claimed that Michelangelo's 'The Night' was her inspiration, and called the piece 'David'. The camera was positioned to give viewers the feeling of being next to him. In accepting to do what was an obviously provocative project, was he making a calculated choice to add to his legend?

Calculated or not, he keeps on pushing the boundaries. In 2005, he became the first footballer to release his very own fragrance. It is entitled 'Instinct'. Impeccably designed, as you might expect, the logo curves the initials dvb (david victoria beckham) over the guardian angel motif he has tattooed on his back as protection for his children. Even something as masculine as an aftershave has to be rooted back to the family man. In the advert for Instinct, which is inevitably accompanied by a suitably smouldering photograph, the Beckham message is emphasized with a selection of words: Storm, defy, fury, tempest, faith, calm, truth, control, peace. These may represent – depending on your level of cynicism – themes of his life, or merely an open invitation for ridicule. He remains a figure of both adulation and fun.

Fame is a notoriously fickle mistress, but the glare of the spotlight hasn't dimmed. Not many celebrities in any walk of life are so consistently on public display. Even actors take some time out between films, or musicians between records. Politicians tend to have a limited shelf life. Beckham, even if he is injured or taking time out during the close season, manages to stay centre stage.

Although the phenomenon means the footballer is sometimes underrated, Beckham would not have sustained the manic interest in his life had he been a mundane player of unexceptional ability. Without the football he'd have been a model. A face. But not an international superstar who makes waves all over the planet.

August 2006 marks a decade since he began his epic journey. Ten years since he took his first major step into the national consciousness in England with a wondergoal. We were stunned by the exceptional sight of a 21-year-old prospect executing a perfect chip from the half way line. As it sailed into the net he marked himself out as something a bit special. Even Pele, the godfather of the beautiful game, never quite managed that.

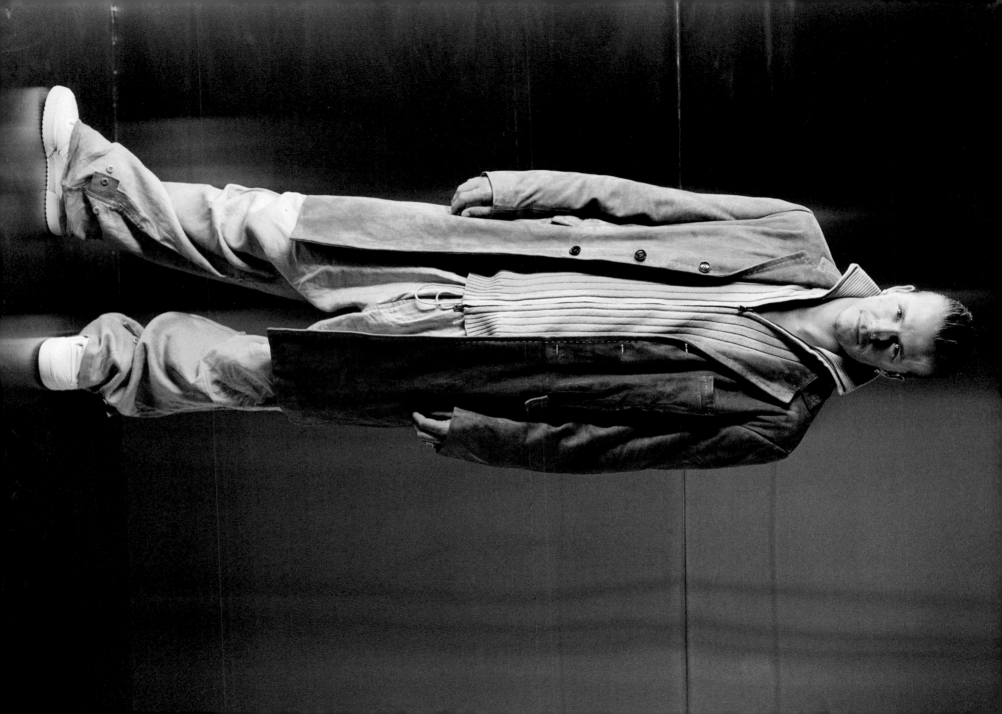

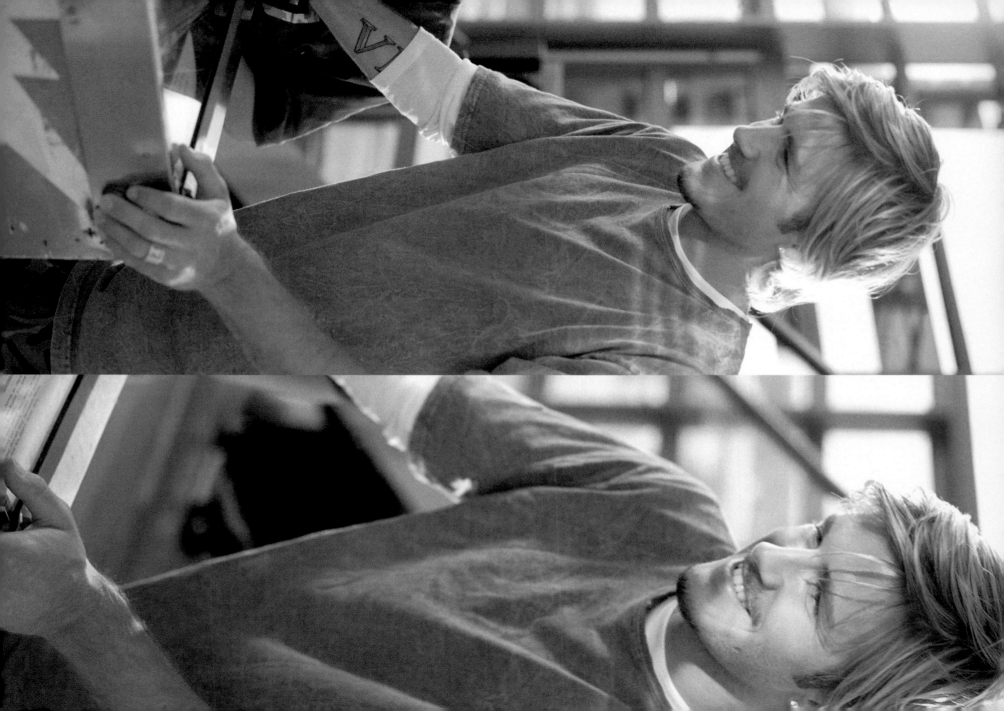

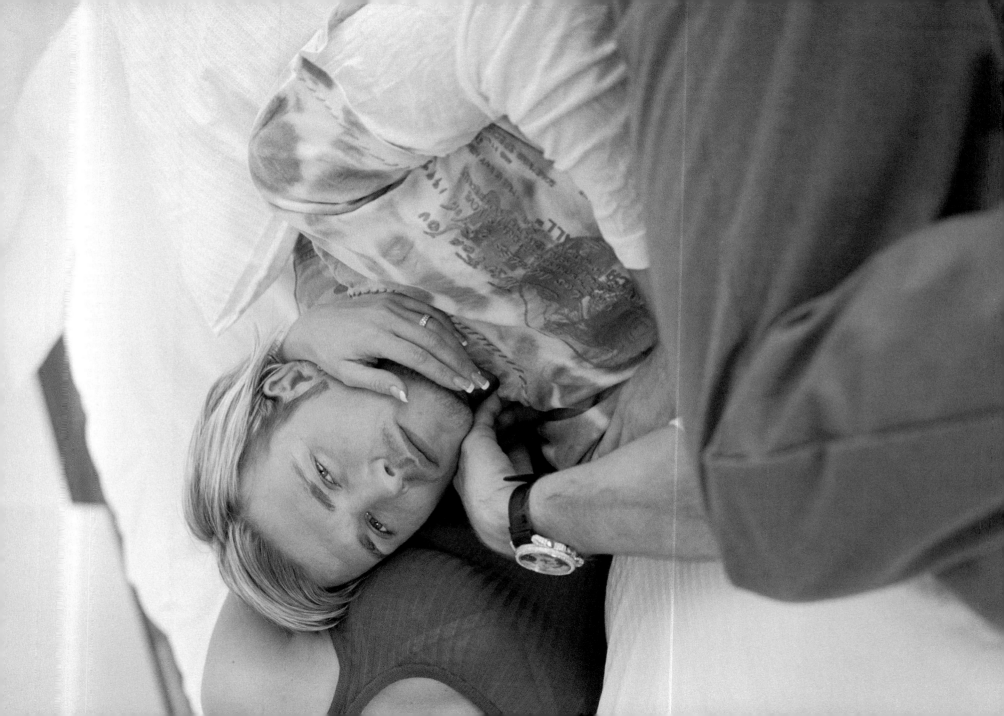

DEAN FREEMAN has achieved critical acclaim photographing major cultural figures, including sporting icons and musicians. In recent years the huge sales of his high-profile books have cemented his reputation for creative vision in the arts, photography and design. His work has been exhibited internationally and acquired by public and private collectors around the world.

AMY LAWRENCE began writing on football for *The Observer* in the same year David Beckham came to prominence with *that* goal from the half way line. Always a world football enthusiast, she has covered three European Championships and is looking forward to her fourth World Cup in Germany.

First published in Great Britain in 2006
by Weidenfeld & Nicolson
10 9 8 7 6 5 4 3 2 1

Text copyright © Amy Lawrence 2006
Pictures copyright © Dean Freeman 2006
Design and layout © Weidenfeld & Nicolson 2006

All rights reserved. No part of this publication may be reproduced, stored in a retrieval system, or transmitted, in any form or by any means, electronic, mechanical, photocopying, recording or otherwise, without the prior permission of both the copyright owner and the above publisher.

The right of the copyright holders to be identified as the authors of this work has been asserted in accordance with the Copyright, Designs and Patents Act 1988.

A CIP catalogue record for this book is available from the British Library.
ISBN-13: 978 0 297 85143 1
ISBN-10: 0 297 85143 8

Printed and bound in Italy

Design director: David Rowley
Designed by Jean-Michel Dentand
Design assistance by Joanna Cannon

Weidenfeld & Nicolson
The Orion Publishing Group Ltd
Wellington House
125 Strand
London, WC2R 0BB

The Orion Publishing Group's policy is to use papers that are natural, renewable and recyclable products and made from wood grown in sustainable forests. The logging and manufacturing processes are expected to conform to the environmental regulations of the country of origin.